Art All Around Us

SLAM POETRY AND STREET PERFORMANCE

Ezra E. Knopp

CREATED BY Humans

Published in 2026 by The Rosen Publishing Group, Inc.
2544 Clinton Street, Buffalo, NY 14224

First Edition

Editor: Greg Roza
Designer: Michael Flynn

Photo Credits: Cover s8/Shutterstock.com; (series background) Yuliya Chsherbakova/Shutterstock.com; p. 5 Eugenio Marongiu/Shutterstock.com; p. 6 https://commons.wikimedia.org/wiki/File:Mosaic_depicting_street_musicians,_signed_by_Dioskourides_of_Samos,_it_was_found_in_the_so-called_Villa_of_Cicero_near_the_ancient_city_of_Pompeii,_Naples_National_Archaeological_Museum_(14817365351).jpg; p. 7 Gilles Paire/Shutterstock.com; p. 9 North Wind Picture Archives/Alamy; p. 10 Old Town Tourist/Shutterstock.com; p. 11 https://commons.wikimedia.org/wiki/File:Pieter_Angillis_-_Covent_Garden_-_Google_Art_Project.jpg; p. 13 cabuscaa/Shutterstock.com; p. 14 (left) Oscar M Sanchez/Shutterstock.com; p. 14 (right) Yatzek Photography/Shutterstock.com; p. 15 (top left) Anna Jurkovska/Shutterstock.com; p. 15 (top right) Smolina Marianna/Shutterstock.com; p. 15 (bottom) Eugenio Marongiu/Shutterstock.com; p. 17 Aleksandar Todorovic/Shutterstock.com; p. 18 (left) https://commons.wikimedia.org/wiki/File:Tracy_Chapman_3.jpg; p. 18 (right) Christian Bertrand/Shutterstock.com; p. 19 (left) Andrea Raffin/Shutterstock.com; p. 19 (right) L Paul Mann/Shutterstock.com; p. 21 Stanislaw1999/Shutterstock.com; p. 23 lev radin/Shutterstock.com; p. 25 Bjoern Deutschmann/Shutterstock.com; p. 27 Finn stock/Shutterstock.com; p. 28 Kitreel/Shutterstock.com; p. 29 Jose Calsina/Shutterstock.com.

Cataloging-in-Publication Data
Names: Knopp, Ezra E.
Title: Slam poetry and street performance / Ezra E. Knopp.
Description: Buffalo, NY : Created by Humans, an imprint of Rosen Publishing, 2026. | Series: Art all around us | Includes glossary and index.
Identifiers: ISBN 9781534552845 (pbk.) | ISBN 9781534552852 (library bound) | ISBN 9781534552869 (ebook)
Subjects: LCSH: Poetry--Juvenile literature. | Poetry--Authorship--Juvenile literature. | Performance art--Juvenile literature.
Classification: LCC PN1031.K655 2026 | DDC 808.1--dc23

Manufactured in the United States of America

CPSIA Compliance Information: Batch #CWCBH26. For Further Information contact Rosen Publishing at 1-800-237-9932.

CONTENTS

ART ON THE CORNER

If you live in a city or large town, you may have seen people performing on the streets or in parks or other public areas. Many street performers play music. Street musicians are sometimes called buskers. If you like their music, you might drop a dollar into their guitar case. That's to say thanks for showing off your talent and making the day more enjoyable!

Why would anyone want to stand on a busy street corner or subway station to entertain passing people? Is it for the dollars people may give them in passing? Is it to show off talent? It's both these reasons and more!

It can be surprising to turn a corner on your way to school or work and come across musicians! It can be nice to stop and listen and watch for a bit.

LONG, LONG AGO . . .

People have been performing for others in public since ancient times. This includes the ancient Greeks, Romans, Chinese, Japanese, and Africans. In ancient Greece, almost all performances were held outside, and roaming groups of performers were common as well. The themes of Greek street performers included religion, **philosophy**, and political **satire**.

Music, dance, and storytelling have long been important cultural elements in African countries. In west Africa, a griot is a historian and storyteller. They tell stories from the past to keep them alive in the culture. They are talented people who entertain and teach **spectators**.

These three men from Burkina Faso, Africa, are griots. They are retelling a family's history with words, rhythm, and music.

Roman Street Performers

Reports from ancient Rome tell of a wide range of street performers—musicians, dancers, storytellers, jugglers, painters, teachers, fortune tellers, and sword swallowers!

MINSTRELS AND TROUBADOURS

During the Middle Ages in Europe (roughly from 500 to 1500), traveling performers were an important source of news and cultural values. They traveled from town to town to entertain people, tell stories, and make a living. They entertained nobles and regular people alike. They brought news and **gossip** from neighboring communities.

During this time, several types of performer roles came to be. Musicians and poets who sang songs and told stories from the past were called minstrels. Troubadours were lyric poets who had great freedom of speech. Many troubadour poems have survived because they were recorded in songbooks.

Jugglers and acrobats became common forms of street art during the Middle Ages.

THE BUSKING BOOM

The **Industrial Revolution** began in England in the late 1700s, and this led to greater ease of travel for street musicians. Street performers included musicians and actors, but also acrobats, magicians, dancers, puppeteers, **organ grinders**, living statues, and more. This increase in performers in urban areas led to the first laws regarding street performers.

The term "busking" was first used to refer to street performers attempting to make money around 1850.

Covent Garden

Covent Garden is an area of London where busking has long been popular with performers and spectators. An outdoor market was set up there in 1830, and it became a wildly popular and crowded spot for buskers. In time, performers would **audition** for property owners in Covent Garden to earn the chance of performing there. Today, Covent Gardens is still a popular place to see street performers of all kinds.

BUSKING TODAY

Street performing is still a lively artform in towns and cities around the world. You're sure to see musicians playing guitars and other portable instruments on street corners, subway stations, city parks, and more. But, thanks to modern **technology**, busking is a whole new game now! Some performers use cashless smart technology to accept **donations** from spectators. Social media allows street performers to reach far more people than ever before.

We no longer need traveling minstrels to bring us news and gossip. We have the internet for that! However, in many countries street performing has become a way to spread political messages or to **protest** something.

Busking can be like a job for serious musicians. They try to perform every day.

TYPES OF STREET PERFORMERS

musicians

actors

jugglers

magicians

dancers

THE CHALLENGES OF BUSKING

Finding success as a street performer can be difficult. It can be hard to make a living that way. Even when a busker isn't performing for money, there can be **challenges**.

Busking is against the law in some places. Some cities have special areas for street performers, such as Covent Garden. Busking is allowed in New York City subway stations, but not on trains. Some areas expect performers to have a permit before they can draw an audience.

Traveling to locations and lugging equipment (such as instruments, costumes, and props) can cause problems, especially for lone performers. Weather can be a problem. So can parking.

Street performers sometimes need to compete for busking locations or for the times when most people are passing by.

NOTABLE BUSKERS

You've probably heard of some of the following performers. They all began their careers as buskers!

Tracy Chapman

Beck

Ed Sheeran

Jewel

Famous Irish actor Pierce Brosnan, known for playing English movie spy James Bond, started his acting career as a street performer. He was a fire eater!

WHAT IS SLAM POETRY?

You're probably familiar with the written art of poetry. Slam poetry is something different. It's a form of poetry that's spoken or performed in front of an audience. Many slam poetry gatherings are held in coffee shops, libraries, auditoriums, and even on the street.

Like many poems, slam poems are often brimming with personal emotions—anger, fear, pride, joy, and more. They may have a political theme or may be a form of protest. Slam poets are free to let their emotions flow in front of an audience, creating an intensely thought-provoking experience for spectators.

It's called "slam" poetry because it's loud, emotional, and in your face, much like street performance itself.

THE SLAM MOVEMENT

Slam poetry began in Chicago in the early 1980s. Poet Marc Kelly Smith felt local poetry readings had become stale. He created a weekly "poetry slam" where any poet could perform. Random audience members were chosen to judge each poem on a scale of 0 to 10. The poet with the highest score was the night's winner.

Poetry slams grew in popularity and spread around the world. The movement even has its own notable artists. Saul Williams is a talented rapper, musician, actor, dancer, and poet. He's won many slam competitions and has appeared in several movies about slam poetry.

The World Slam Poetry Championship (WPSO) is the largest annual poetry slam in the world! It's held in a different city each year.

Saul Williams

SLAM RULES!

Most poetry slams have rules. Rules may vary from one slam to another, but some general rules are often followed.

1. Poems must be original creations.
2. You may allow another speaker to read your poem if you have a disability or impairment.
3. Poems should not go over three minutes. Time begins when you start talking.
4. Anyone can perform regardless of race, age, gender, education, or disability.
5. The poem may not include sexist, racist, homophobic, or transphobic comments that are meant to belittle or offend people.
6. No props or costumes may be used.
7. No musical instruments may be used. Poets are allowed to sing, clap, hum, and make other sound effects.
8. You can read your work from a notebook or phone.

Slam gatherings and competitions are welcoming events open to everyone.

HOW TO GET STARTED

Does the thought of performing in public interest you? How do you get started? First you need to identify your artistic skills and build upon them. Are you taking music lessons? That's a great start! So is taking acting classes, learning to juggle, and practicing public speaking. Don't forget to practice!

There may be local artistic groups you can join. That's a good way to start networking. That means meeting people who may be able to help you in the future. You can also search for good busking spots in your community. Look for other buskers and make a note of where they perform.

There are so many ways to display your creativity to the public.

THE STREET PERFORMER IN YOU

Now that you know all about street performances and slam poetry, do you think you have what it takes to perform for an audience of **pedestrians**? Are you ready to haul your instrument and props to a busy street corner? Can you handle a few boos in the middle of a performance? If you said yes, you may have what it takes to be a street performer!

Can you see yourself participating in an artistic street performance? Which talent do you like the most?

GLOSSARY

audition: A trial performance to witness an entertainer's skills.

challenge: Something that makes something else hard to do.

donation: A gift of money to a charity or for a performance.

gossip: Information about a person's life that may or may not be true.

Industrial Revolution: An era of social and economic changes, starting in the late 1700s in England, that marked advances in technology and science.

organ grinder: A street performer who used a barrel organ (a large music box) to entertain pedestrians. Organ grinders turned a handle to make music on a barrel organ.

pedestrian: A person traveling by walking.

philosophy: The study of the basic ideas about knowledge, truth, right and wrong, religion, and the nature and meaning of life.

protest: A complaint, objection, or display of unwillingness or disapproval.

satire: Something meant to make fun of and show the weaknesses of human nature or a particular person.

spectator: Someone who is watching something.

technology: A method that uses science to solve problems and the tools used to solve those problems.

FOR MORE INFORMATION

BOOKS

DK staff. *Music and How It Works: The Complete Guide for Kids.* London, UK: DK Children, 2020.

Wall, Thom, et. al. *Juggling: What It Is and How to Do It.* Philadelphia, PA: Modern Vaudeville Press, 2021.

WEBSITES

Covent Garden Performers Association
www.coventgardenperformers.com
Visit this website to learn more about Covent Gardens and the numerous street performers found there.

StreetJelly
www.streetjelly.com
If you're visiting New York City and want to catch some inspiring street performances, check out this website! Includes links to videos of street performers.

Publisher's note to educators and parents: Our editors have carefully reviewed these websites to ensure that they are suitable for students. Many websites change frequently, however, and we cannot guarantee that a site's future contents will continue to meet our high standards of quality and educational value. Be advised that students should be closely supervised whenever they access the internet.

INDEX